NESPOLA

By the same author:

Aril Wire (2018)

Totality (2022)

NESPOLA

ANDERS VILLANI

Nespola
Recent Work Press
Canberra, Australia

ISBN: 9781764106887 (paperback)

A catalogue record for this book is available from the National Library of Australia

Cover image: © Tyler Arnold, 2026
Internal images: © Tyler Arnold, 2026
Author photograph by Cherry Collins
Cover design: Recent Work Press
Set by Recent Work Press

This project has been assisted by the Australian Government through Creative Australia, its principal arts investment and advisory body.

recentworkpress.com

SS

Contents

You forests of my childhood, should I
Come to you now, the same peace as ever?

—Hölderlin, 'Home,' translated by Michael Hamburger

...and sometimes, from fantasy comes union.

—Rumi, 'A Children's Game,' translated by Coleman Banks

...move your mind, move your mind, it's gonna come to nothing.

—Eiffel 65, 'Move Your Body'

On the Rise

All morning, the brothers work
their father. They break him—he abandons
his alone time, loads the wagon, drives to the courts.
Rain will break the bushfire soon.
The atmosphere knows. Whipped as its heat
prepares, resists. As its clouds avalanche.
They drill. A northerly wind swirls
the ball—wind's ballpoint—and neither
boy can middle it, make better
than jammed or remote contact.
They're thirsty, but clouds of parched
wasps no-go-zone the fountains.
They're sucking in air; it's rubber. It's dust
from clay so thin and dry they're running on oil.
Their father could tell them
to give up, could say it's alright,
he'll take them home, fix them iced drinks.
That would arm them. It has to come from them.
Knowing this—more provocation.
So their father feeds. *Take it on*
the rise, take it early, Agassi it, play your way in.
Frame. Spray. Reactive and impotent
the way the little brother last holidays tried to
punch waves back to the far ocean.
Their father removes his shirt. He turns, glossy, towards the smoke
half of the sky to get the balls, contorting
rubber through the basket slats. From a way off
the big brother watches the little one slip
under the net when a gust parachutes it, racquet
cocked, aglow as if the graphite
were just cast. As if what middles
the man's back is soft, molten, setting.

Catharsis

In the first still, you're in a taxi,
carrying a beer bottle. Left index finger
down the bottle's neck. Cork.
Wick. In the CCTV footage—King Street—figures
shoal and break and one, face in hands,
kneels. In the second still, you're a prophet
carrying the shirt someone tore off you in shards, or you tore off yourself.
Sinewed torso. Zero-shaved head. Fists
flowering with parchment. A prophet who has
no idea where he is or what he's doing
and has ergo attained presence. Rage not rage
in that it bears no differentiation, like agony so great it un-names you,
like care, like your nightmares as a boy
—thumb-sucking little—of a man peeling *nespola*
eyes, like glass off a mirror. In the old epic
those nightmares woke me in the top bunk, and I wake
this waking the dawn after they've summoned
E and me into the suite of revelation, declared her a carrier
of the gene. How seldom the blessed
ask: how much of myself, to save
myself, can I destroy? Where'd the bottle go?
Forget what they allege. That's here. That's all in the report.
Then again, what changes whether you tell me
this or that tale of shattering? What genre
of brother would I be if my love were contingent on your
not becoming your terrors? Hidden
tape rolls—shall we watch? In this footage, I sleep sweet.
The *nespole* I pick off our tree aren't eyes, but ripe fruit, but the
blossom I am while you're still
at Woolamai in 1997, treading
above a giant manta, aware it carries you,
blank boy, liquid, black elegance.

Amateurism (or Youth)

boy a work in progress /
not *work* as in *exercise*
though this too / boy smoke
bees dream / boy's name

sidereal / guttered candle / more
resistance than it's worth
resisting /

not *work* as in *piece of*

though this too / boy voice
assonantly / boy's name a wrecking
ball meek as cannons
children climb / limbs cold

or hot as the bronze / scrape
-hoard under nails
for after / not *work* as in *master*

though this too / this more

/ boy the transplanting of

feijoas from a front yard
to be slabbed into buckets / this fruit
in wait / boy voice

/ boy the confidence of one

word that won't resist / one

heap of salt in a cast-iron pan
                    nearer   /   nearer the mercury
at which it corrodes   /   purifies   /

not *work* as in *absence*
though this too   /   this less   /   boy
              progress's ghost   /   boy behind

the name in the water   /

Arranged Marriage

The family buys him
a young bride, gold as a queen's anklets.

The union founders. He can't
feed himself. Why did the family think he could feed her?

Some days, he's walking
and Earth liquifies. And the family
wanted him to dress to the nines and jaunt the esplanade with her

on his arm, unclip and coil
the leash and swim her
tired in the bay, snapper-dawned, parrot-fish-dusked.

When he does eat, runes
razored into his eyebrows, picking
the pantry locks after midnight, why did the family

think she wouldn't feed in his room
on vomit with a lover's hunger, a lover's relish?
Lick the dirt outside his window

clean of the tuna-can oil he pours from bed?
Did the family not think?

They did. They thought of what his bride could do for him.
Of how she'd been bred. How she'd been finished.

But, thinking of themselves, they didn't consider his

having to look at
the look she gives, won't stop giving.

Loquat Giant

Nonna asks for *nespole* in her favourite bowl
(the bowl that scuffs our fingers, like pumice).

Frontiering to the tree, we find a praying mantis.
Fine jam on our fingers. Balm on them. Interred
and mourned. We bury our hands to the wrist in soil

a truck dumped in our carport and I licked one night.
One of us radicchio, one turmeric—harvest
and offcut. Are we,

asks a lover decades later, near horses wild for their carrots,
going to hurt each other like I

or you want? But pain is just one form of lush
staring that disappears. Where
am I? Mantis jam. Mum pulsing the gas like a piano pedal: this nocturne as bowl

buckling lawn, shuttlecock pinging off strings. Swoosh
of helicoptered graphite.
Remember when you saw the world?

To reach the best *nespole*, you climb my shoulders.
Shake soil from your hands and caterpillars from the branches
onto my cheeks—how waves

of their panic crest, capillary this waiting.
Horses, wild for carrots. Manes blonde as the hair I tease

from a drain and hold through a Zoom call
—a seed, a bulb. Here's memory, digging up
the giant it slays. After prayer, Nonna recalls eating burnt

-butter horses on her island; they smelled of figs,
of *nespole* they chewed to jam in her hand.

Manifesto

He gathers every leaf
he observes with a spider
egg sac fused to it.

He burns these leaves, sacs, on the stove,
how his mother liquifies
eggplant in blue lakes of flame.

He finds his body's palest zones.
Sun-orphaned. Abyss
of wrist, etcetera.

He burns them with an asthma inhaler
until scars rise like fishkill.
He works lazily.

His brother's mattress, on cinderblocks, dusty
enough to write on
but not for this to be legible.

He piles reasons here.
While the wind chime
forgets the wind.

Night of the Royal Melbourne Show

Sugar through their blood
and flannel, the boys see the night.
They binge sour lollies. Their sick
budgie pecks her grit. The Sea
-Monkeys in the glass on the desk aren't coming alive.
Top-bunk boy strokes his nipples
and says they'll catch tadpoles.
He caresses his flanks—or she does.
Alanis. From earlier, when they were parking
in the showgrounds lot and her song came on—I'm brave

but I'm chicken…Shit. Shit was the next word
and the radio beeped it out. Made it shh
as if she were shooshing herself, and him, a girl
let go her helium balloon, which joined the others, so many
redfin shoaling upstream to the sun, Dad cut the engine,

and in the time it took to unbuckle and get out he forgot
what everything meant and—a game
cartridge resetting—remembered it
but worse, harsher—a judge had come

alive in the radio's blackout. The Show couldn't touch him.
It was for babies. And his little baby
brother's black hair plastered to his head with a washcloth and water
hurt and angered him, makes him squeamish to
think, pity, smell, in this dark
pleasure as gods and Alanis watch.
At dawn with yabby nets they dragnet the pond in the park down the road.
They cage hundreds in a fish tank.
Soon, the almost-frogs want freedom,
half-bodies pecking the glass.

Deer Knife

When life hides behind the mulch
    of what lives, can they expect more
            than this refusal to hold each other in the open?

Lemongrass floss between molars,
    you wish for foxes. You tell me you don't wish for them
            any novel way, no way—no
word—being more or less novel. You wish for

    foxes in the impossible neutral, piss baroquely on
            the coal heap around the young lime
whose illness we've yet to diagnose
    though we yoke answers to the answer.

            At the rim of the secret's crater, you balance
on your head and imagine water
    to slant, migrating, because it must. But listen: the Pacific
            gull that slit childhood? Bombing the ocean, never resurfacing?

It did resurface. What hides from us
    leaks what we do not see. Brothers speaking together
            underwater. Brothers holding each
other's breath.

I have hidden from you. Keep counting. Keep grinding
    memory's deer knife through gritty, mulched
            soil to clean it. When we hold each other, may it not
be the afterlife. Here is a public

garden. A body lighting the lemongrass
    the breeze wicks from airy, flax clothes
            as hunger wicks a fox from another den.

Polyglots

Now the weeds must be cut back
I can put you in my bath
with a stranger who read auras, thin

broth of night, doghair galoshed around the
outdoor tub's ornate wrought-iron feet,

citronella-oil lily pads. Through mine came: *calm.*
I didn't ask if they meant *shock*,

just knew and in-chanted it. We're all polyglots

in breath. Do you remember at school, the parade

my friends threw declaring

that when you were older, they'd marry you?
Query a slow heart. Dispute praise the way safety
-crazed skin disputes ice

baths with discipline enough and it's rest, it's
safety, it's cadence firm

as a lily pad. Now the weeds must grow back, beloved,
do I read right? We're calm, our embrace consensus

that embrace would put us under.
We're shocked on nights we hear, Strangers,
it is that gust, it is that chance.

Plums

And I have something to tell you
Which not even I must hear.
—Yiannis Ritsos, 'A Small Invitation,' translated by Kimon Friar

The wide back window
reflects pool, *nespola* tree, green pool
fence, sky, back fence and plum
-tree canopy that is birdfeed and the neighbours'
Sarajevo grappa.
Sometimes the window reflects a child, foraging
blowflies from the track and crushing
these desiccated roses to sky
-write on the frame varnish, war-paint cheekbones,
shotput into pool, trumpet
this gift for the ripples of raw-yellow light, this salvation.
Sometimes the window reflects the child's thoughts. Treasure
maps of the yard. School crushes. Cats svelting through pool fence.
Rosellas in beveled sky dreaming
of *nespole* they'd feast on, grappa
plums, if their wings found in them
a slower, alighting, gear.
The neighbours' war songs.
Secrets not even the child must hear.
Look: behind green fence, behind sky, the child stares
harder, into two slit blue
plums of a thing
without name, source, destiny, bowels—stares through
and as window, reflecting one pool. It lasts
moments. It is for a birth's width the grammar
and fear that distills someone
alight away awake.

Wallpaper

I stick shut scissors in the doorhandle's cavity and twist. He's on his bed on his knees. Pressing bamboo forest, manna-gum forest, seaweed forest, to the wall. Peel-and-stick, like book contact. One idea is that living in a partial wilderness will centre him. Which do I like? The promontory water iron stained the ochre of dead fir needles at the river mouth this weekend, where the sea told me it was acceptable to love him as fascination. As hunger. Lemons for ash. Black glass for sun. Feverish cat for bottlebrush. His room bare save for a bed and a nightstand. Nothing on the nightstand but the nice cologne he stole from me ten years ago. It's unused. Go back: my hand trembles the doorhandle, and he and his mates laugh as he denies stealing it, everyone looking at it. A dozen lungs stained sweet with it. How meth smoke smells of aniseed. How I backed out of the room into a monsoonal waiting. Why has he kept it? One idea is that he's kept an unsigned note. But now, invisible as the best poisons, it's a forest. Centre lost in the edges. Had he worn it every day until it ran dry, a teen chaining a carton of menthols while Mum bones fish, I'd have said, That's your penance. That's my cowardice lost in patience. It's time to admit that at the river mouth, beneath seaweed, gulls lay dead, hundreds, agape, gum-pink, and I reached through one to his hair.

Ceilings

Tennis Australia invites ten boys
to a week-long camp
all expenses paid
for the country's best twelve-and-unders
they stay in twin rooms
at the Richmond Hill Hotel
near Melbourne Park
where they train from morning to night
working out in the gym Australian Open players use
Hewitt's favourite elliptical Tommy Hass's
rowing machine the medicine balls
Hingis and her Mum loop to each other
running time trials around
the Rod Laver Arena concourse
which looks bigger when it's empty and feels
bigger when it has no smell
of chips and ball felt and sunscreen
it's their kingdom every morning
before picking up a racquet they stretch for thirty minutes
they do the same after setting their racquets down
for lunch they eat catered chicken
and mayo sandwiches and drink Mountain Blast
Powerades from ice buckets
it's good weather every day the nets
are crisp they crack
new cans of balls every few hours
for dinner they eat at reasonable restaurants in the city
the coaches five good-looking men
wear leather jackets and aftershave
wear watches but not glasses and have wallets
bulging with cards and receipts the coaches
make the wait staff blush

not by saying anything
inappropriate just by having something
one of the boys has never known
a man to have something lazy
but not lazy at all they are driven
and focused men the coaches
AIS coaches Junior Davis Cup captains
fitness trainers to the stars
one of them used to hit with Dokic at Slams
before she started playing for Yugoslavia
the first time any of the boys has heard of that place
what the coaches have the boy thinks
in bed later as he rubs himself is ease
not a wisp of doubt and the boy
has never known men like that men
who seem to have won some tournament
to be always winning it on Thursday
they do three hours of fitness tests
vertical leap beep test suicide sprints push-ups
standing long jump the idea
is to find out what sort of athletes these men will become
how far they'll be able to push
their bodies before they break or hit
ceilings of the ten boys
one will earn millions and beat Federer
one the best of them now
will play college in America and hustle
a meagre living on the doubles circuit
back injuries will snuff out one's generational promise
one will think of this camp
at a strange time at a campsite when they
tow a huge dead manna gum into the centre
it's afternoon or early evening
start chainsawing the tree into pieces
they can lift or at least roll for the fire and from
the dead tree's hollow core emerge

dozens maybe hundreds of spiders
huge and grey like the warm dark
nest from which blades cut them
and it's every spider for itself
while the group screams rushes to zip up tents and swags
and the dogs lose their wits
the rest of the ten boys may the rest live
on amicable terms with the game once
a day the boys do a
morale-building exercise
a bit of fun
karaoke the one where you fall
back and they catch you
on Friday on the school-classroom carpet
of the upper Rod Laver concourse
the boys stand facing a concrete pylon ten metres away
on the whistle
each boy closes his eyes
runs as fast as he can towards the pylon
stopping on the next whistle
it's about trust the coaches say
closing your eyes and trusting
you're in safe hands
one by one the boys go
on the whistle stop on the whistle
everyone cheers and high-fives
tennis is a lonely sport the coaches say
tomorrow is match-play day you'll all
be competing against each other
to see who makes the squad
to play the New Zealand boys in Auckland
so enjoy this mateship support
each other trust each other
you're all Aussies well one of you is
Tasmanian the last boy
takes his mark the whistle blows it takes

a long time or maybe not so long
a few minutes at most
for the coaches to understand that words
of reassurance will not do it
that *come on you can do it* from the other boys fans
his refusal's flames
that subjecting
him to this much longer might scar him
he's flushed definitely crying
they let him walk with his eyes open a crack
straighten his hat pat his head
the other boys high-fiving quiet wanting
to laugh knowing not to knowing
they've seen something
the coaches hadn't planned in the afternoon
in a conference room with
views of the courts Todd Woodbridge
talks hard work motivation
takes photos with them quotes Muhammad Ali
he is the nicest man with
the nicest hair like a boy's hair still

Compassionate Grounds

Nausea ransoms hour twelve
of the second flight. It wants the Dramamine
forgotten in Melbourne. In Hong Kong
in vain we searched circling the dark

empty terminal for hours, masked remains apocalypse
had left breathing to sing of it.
In *Planet of the Apes*, the human has just sung
his hatred loose. Something is going on. Humans

singing at me through headphones and pointing, flailing
at you pale in the aisle, outside the toilet
on your back. Attendants chorusing. Let's pretend it's
got nothing to do with blood sugar.

Let's pretend it's next week. A bright Chicago
operating theatre. It's after, when you need me, when we walk
the terminal—a belief, memory-old, that I love
no one—and see what opens. Who comes.

A curtain opens. Your chorus. They've snuck
you croissants from first class, mini
jars of Bonne Maman. Apricot, fig. Are you sugared? What
else, little cub? Let's pretend my government permit

wasn't to leave, but to become human. Charlton
commandeers a horse just in time
for the surf

of catastrophe—Lady Liberty—to sing in him.
No one acts like this anymore.
So forced, so blatantly acting. As though the act
masks a captive real.

Log

9:30pm. Day 1.

Drain 1: 30ml, raspberry coulis

Drain 2: 23ml, raspberry coulis

Drain 3: 30ml, raspberry coulis

Drain 4: 18ml, raspberry coulis, faint custard head.

Ulupna Island

Red river, red river,
Slow flow heat is silence
—T.S. Eliot, 'Virginia'

Lovers flee to their river beach on the state border. Since they last came, before lockdown, steel power poles have streaked one side of the highway. The logs on the obsolete side are lineless. Cruciform. NO SWIMMING signs—water starchy with blue-green algae.

They make camp. For days, they become the beach. In her notebook, she nothings *light hiding in the lit /current a colt (my new chest unlatches its pen)*. His gaze

follows galahs across to the island, khaki canvas tent, underwear on a river-gum branch. If she were to suck water through the fibres of that underwear, she would know the soap's trace like her skin's oil. Because he's in the tent on the island and has fled the island, it's the measure of forgetting. Because measure

is rupture, because forgetting is memory's electricity, because the history of the universe is the history of silence scarcely and spectacularly surrendering, when it's mutest, the bush cracks. River cracks while the bush echoes. Then it's done. Over the island bank—cliffed by erosion—

two animals have flown in. Through koala binoculars, they watch one thrash ashore. White Kevlar armour—exoskeleton. Boar dog. The second, a kangaroo the dog was hunting, the river holds. Baby brother camped in the involuntary ward at the back of a linen closet deadbolted from within, fleeing, rigid as a

starched blanket. Currents deny the roo either bank—either state. Algae logs taunt it. Why dash downriver after what they can't rescue? Undress and streak

as if the river wouldn't drown them, touch disembowel them? Because they're decent. Because self-blame, too, is a beach. The roo's strong—it won't sink. How long grief can lack the object that floats, muzzle skied, past it. How long ghosts can languish living-haunted.

Question, Annulled by its Force

It's not rape though,
I tell him. It's a game. Extreme-sport
trust. He could say it denounces
rape in the most forceful way possible.
Whatever phrasing he needs.
We do more ketamine. The chestnuts
he brought up earlier, the chestnuts he
and his ex foraged and braised
that turned out to be delicious
analogues—in hospital, were doctors
pumping chestnuts from his ex's stomach?
No: the almost, the proximity,
was the foreignness—the more foreign, the more
intimate the ruse. I'm trying different ways
to explain desire for me and he won't grasp it.
He's holding my legs weakly on a white rug.
Like plum drying, he's turning mineral,
meek. What is a game if not anything
all parties agree is a game? And sure, those
not-chestnuts nearly killed his ex. I concede that
taking someone's freedom takes
no courage unless they offer it. If he accepts, has me
convinced, he'll hear how pure
consent can sound. Isn't that his ecstasy?
Not stripping me of power but telling me, *Shut up*
and *Wield it*, pinning me in its dark lake.
Most real things aren't true—he said that himself
in the text that made me drive to him,
believe we could have fun, believe he could do this
despite his ex, this expert at hiding
the rule that he must keep himself hidden.
So. Will he play?

Valour

If he were angrier, it would be better
for them. She would like that more.
Want him in a way she can't anymore.

They can't be in the car anymore. Camp in a *gravel*
dump—what the app calls it—behind an oval
off the Hume, near Melbourne.

Black cockatoos laugh at sunset.

At 4 a.m., a car whips in. Gravel fireworks, high
beams catching the apple-green tent fly. He imagines

they can see him. Silhouetted, as his toes
steal glances at her heels pumiced
smooth by seabed. The lovers—

frenzied in that focused, eloquent, ice way.
She trusted that psycho who pranks her at work
threatens him

threatens to rape his kids—
she ate his come. Lent him four grand.

And she won't loan him? Won't trust him? Is she going to
shit   why'd they take this exit?

Boot in the door if the toilet's locked.
Go on the ground. Go on the ground, dog.

Where's his pipe? It's not under the seat and if she doesn't
find it in ten seconds. Where's that fifty bucks?

Awake now, she holds him. He holds
the wrench from the vestibule. A man who longs to run
clean as boiled water

gums rust off the wrench head. So many addicts
roam in couples like birds, he thinks,
outside sadness, retooled for murder.

Suspicions

I'm off work but speak all night about it.
He's a writer. I'm an escort. The cost
of monetising passion.

And returning to passion—to this old
shiraz and gold couch and woodstove
crackle and choke and spit; to the page and what without

forethought bathes it—

how bad is the bleed-through, how flat,
how used the taste, humans being unworthy
of the divisions they worship? Drunk

brag: it began with sex and poetry.
Sister professions, thirst traps—the prime
movers, threats, because they make ideas beautiful.

But—not to be reductive—sex is body and poetry the vain project
of mind to be body. Feel this chill man.

He suspects he's a client. I suspect his poems
no longer get—never got?—what I just gave him,
a real name.

Love Processions

In my novel, we're beyond brothers.
We're twins. You're a princess
in a tower and I'm the hero, selfless, humble
enough to admit I can't save you
as I save you. Novel: you don't remember

verbally, but with quelled grins. Glints
in your adrenals like princesses in a tower.
Real world: I shave your head, my back and sides. Our
greys helix on the sparkly
garage slab and I'm saving you. I don't know
what else to call it. My fatal weakness

is voice. I can't distinguish characters. They all end up boys'
bodies in a pool of
the quest to proliferate myself. To prove worthy
of the cosmos, mustn't you become it? Novel: I collapse
our anguish into one, kill

off anguish of comparison, shortfall, but save
choice particulars, like our respective
claims to anguish. Is that bad art? How secular
to want something so much we could forget we want divinity more.
At 3 am, a pokies machine cycles through lemons and cherries, lands
again on cataclysm. Novel: it never lands,

and the cycling is a sweet wind
my fan gives a princess's face that wakes them.
We sit at the kitchen table in the tower while I dress
the wounds you've stripped. My wounds.
My hero. My swooning double.

Mist

On a skyscraper ledge, falcons near hatching. Lovers run
the livestream all night. Blue
    night light. Under the disco ball

        at the roller rink where he first kissed someone
        (Elise) while holding their
            whole arse, in *Viparita Karani*, she spins her blade wheels

while lymphatic fluid drains. He blades around
her and it's a wheel. Tyre, hub, bearing. Their
    eyes the buffering. Years

        through the hour, mist fledges
        from the gully's foreign slope. Never and nowhere is there
            subtraction. They 69. Mother guards her eggs. You are born

with your eggs, so whose womb had you craved when they fished you, tiny, filling,
from the rainwater tank? She chisels hunks from a salt lamp—the shaker's
    out—to CPR soup. Soon, advent. He cups his god

        -mother's conch to his ear as a child, hears blood
        rivers burst banks, hears peregrinations—that's his darling
            dusting the loft windows—while her soft feet crack

scrub along the Murray to tail a kangaroo who's fallen in,
who's drowning—to save it, to drape its
    lifelessness over them and keep rolling. That peregrines are the fastest beings on Earth

        doesn't awe the lovers, who are faster. It's that the birds' speed
        is focus. Hunting. Evading.
            When will they cut out her ovaries.

Test Conditions

A bright day. Neutral.
You've been lounging, at rest.
They ask if you'd like to do something.
Go to Costa Rica this summer.
Go on a drive to Kinglake
to smell the waterfall. Undress them.
Make toasted-cheese sandwiches.
Attend an anti-war rally.
Pro-war. It doesn't matter.
They're just sounding you out,
gauging your interest. Low pressure.
Low stakes. Your body
says otherwise. Says this is something
you don't want, says it with
your gut, your viced throat.
This precedes your considering
whether you want to do it. The proposal—
its fact, not its substance—
has forced itself upon you, a dead
rabbit down sovereignty's well.
You were rejection-rabid.
Against this poisoning, you weigh
the specifics. But they're compromised.
You're talking yourself into
enduring events that may
be magnificently what you want
if there were neutral assessment room.
Stall, equivocate. No longer
spur-of-the-moment, the proposal
is void. They shouldn't have asked.
Wouldn't trust your yes.
Seeing you react like this over so little

so many times has left them sympathetic,
patient, yet they're not after much,
not much, too much, they know,
a simple answer, and you give it to them
sometimes and it's always no
but sudden, brusque, adamant, *no*
to that bite of their meal
as if their offering you this bite
were a hostile act, an incursion
beyond boundaries you have
to redraw at any cost though maybe
the meal smells excellent, maybe
you do want this balanced
forkful of each component
with the optimal amount of sauce
they've prepared, glad to feed you,
and they have to take you
at your word, but your refusal hurts them
despite its excessiveness
slightly invalidating it, slightly
invalidating their hurt
for which they feel mean, controlling,
though you reassure them they're not,
their feather gesture now a thing
too dense to get into at brunch
except you are in it, appetites
off somewhere. Today—
day feels too leading; there's no day
here—you tell them you're not sure.
You need to think. As if
delaying your answer bought you time
to hone and trust it and not the rabbit
time to decompose. That gentle
valley in your shoulders
is you returning to a bunk bed,
not accepting this return, but returning,

top bunk, *Thomas the Tank* sheets,
returning to where no tyrant can
nail fiats to the door and no speech
can bend you away from the bright
neutral alone from which all
speech is contrivance, departure,
speech like this smoothing over,
this remorse, this making light of,
this promise to do the work, this passing
funk, this laughing off, this going
on a drive, veggie pasties, ponies in a paddock,
this decrying an unjust war,
this happiness, this undressing, this
mineral waterfall scent you
don't know if you don't know
if you don't want.

Rosella Bush

There are no questions
about Bangalore or coding. It's all molasses
irises, mole *stray*
caviar beside my lip, nipples
black as papaya seeds.
But he listens to this. He too nurses breakup wounds.
How my fiancée texted while I filled

a hospital bed—
multiple sclerosis. How that first plunge
of immunosuppressives
imbedded a fatigue
that flits like a cat from its yard.
It is in the yard it is dead
in a foreign yard it is in the yard

a rosella in its jaws. I can see
his lust wants to envelop me. I can see his pity
wants to martyr itself for me in a lustful way, in a way that dilates lust.
Past 2 am, I navigate him.
Have you tasted rosella bush?
He listens to this. He's gentle, as if cool plant
milk flows where blood should, as if he has recoded

himself without anger, forgetting
all the essential lines that must be erased to do that.
I don't ask about his brother though he seems to want that.
Past 2 am, at last, we glimpse
death's face in the glass
that is desire. My
face. No one's. His.

Cones

Silkworm, threading lithe golden
shoulder hair into a shagpile rug
for hours, stripped of nakedness, slick
with vanishing's friction—When have you dreamt?

When you saw the children with silk
        gaits approach, melt to their knees, hands

        drills for the hole from which they pulled dancing
worms and ate parts of them, learning disgust

was a pact, like money, like beauty.
Learning beauty. When have you swum upriver towards
as impossible a source as them?

When you smelled blackberry bush on fire.
When you saw grass threaded through a Persian
cat's shit as silk. When have you moved. When have you not moved.

Movement's silkworms pinned
under orange cones, free halves bulging; the illicitness

of fanning a perch tail still
cool with life. When have you dreamt
                        anything less than your life

that might let you see your life? What silks would you thread

from it if you saw it, the rug asks, the black
-eyebrowed lover asks in a voice message.
Meaning: do this when you touch it.
            Do unto silk as silk does unto silk.

Conspiracy Theorist

It returns like the nettles—
a campaign to peel
authentic from inauthentic.

Eating me out, he's fed
tongue aerobatics
through an earpiece. He actually says that later.
He calls hot showers total
submission, total fusion, then doesn't get

in with himself, drinking
burning water through cloth as he did
as a child as if to corrode
a desire line from liver to free thought. I'm over it.
Indecision. Asceticism. Laughter over ridges. Masculinity this hyper

better build me something.
A bed. Street nettles he whips
into risotto one night and it smells rich, the air
dramatic with bushfire smoke.
I saw him in tears with my cat once.

I saw him, in that embrace on the carpet, glimpse
himself as what he obviously is, not
that it lasted—how could it?
His one solid a wire
rack on which doubt chills.

We join open mouths. Tongues
lazing like tired wrens,
rice drinking itself swollen.

Under the Banner of Heaven

Not many know this path. Gold
-rush dynamite blew it to the river. I promise
not to let the cat out of the bag and he leads me down.
Cut-back blackberry edges us, vehement again.
By the water, in Cuban-heeled boots, he cracks
knuckles while I sit on a river-gum root, roll a spliff.
His boots are heel-deep in mud. It's weird.
He's—how to put it—a warm, safe planet, and distant
moons of that planet. Blue eyes a chemical
reaction that's turning white. To slow that reaction
I ask if he has wine at his house. He does, but
yesterday the good bottle he bought for me
fell off the top of the fridge as he shut the door, a full bottle of red
that fell and shattered against the floor slate
in the future and the past at the same time. *The stationary*
blast of waterfalls, he says in a way that makes clear
he's quoting someone though he doesn't attribute it, and I don't ask
through my throatful of bush bud. He edges
towards the waterline. The mud gives like wet sand.
He's going to keep walking, turn. I've stumbled
into a baptism but won't know until it happens
whether I'm receiving or administering it.
Kookaburras. Once the merlot river had
run its tributaries under the fridge and bins and cupboards
and stained the grouting forever, he woke up,
swept up dark-green glass, laid paper towels,
searched for the mop-and-bucket, found it out under the eaves.
There was something alive in the bucket.
He was in the laundry running water
hot and there it was. *Litoria ewingii*
—brown tree frog. It took surprising force
and surprising gentleness to unstick its feet from the bucket side.

It was the gentlest thing he'd had in his hands save
for a human face. He took it outside, put it in a bird bath
but pulled it out when he realised the shallow water was hot.
He thought he'd boiled it. But, clinging to him,
it told him to take it to the damp soil at the bottom
of the property and release it. He's been peeling
eucalyptus leaves into strips. These fall.
The sex is the least worst in a while. He worships the leotard
under my dress and the lace
under the leotard. We call each other beautiful.
We are beautiful and perfect. We both know
it's just this. He's trying to erase, annul, open, forget
with an abandon I find hot, if grave, given I'm not here
to tend or understand. As he cooks me dinner
we realise we have a mutual friend.
He knows them through the art scene
and I made out with them in LDS church. I pivot
to church stuff. Doubts and certainties he won't fathom.
My dad a bishop. Samoa missions. How I hide
chocolate when Mum visits for fear of upsetting her.
At the limit, blood is lukewarm belief, I tell him.
Later. Very late. He says this or I dream it.
He says, or I dream he says, that the wine bottle
—or I, who caused the bottle's purchase—shattered
another encounter into being. He's somewhere
downstairs. His cat finds him. Releasing the frog
he left the door ajar; the cat got loose,
caught the skink it presents here, tail
detached and decoy-thrashing, face a red jewel.
This comes to me: his thumbs rest on my eyelids
like a biometric scan for a vault (what's in it?) he's convinced
he must but can't access. Beckoning sirens. Coming
tender home to flight. Isn't that you
and God? he asks, or I dream he asks.
I love telling him it's not, he doesn't know either of us.
Voice or dream the decree's wax seal.

He sleep-talks, or I dream he does, Look at the purple
jacaranda bloom. The jacaranda. Look
at it this way: how, if I'm not running, can I reach anywhere?
Laughter either at the pop
kitsch of this question or how it arrows him.
The half-breaths of blackberry breath.
Tonnes and tonnes of wool bedding.
He says, or I dream he says, that the lizard
his cat brings him is alive. All humane paths
lead to the axe butt and he is humane,
he is good. He asks to what degree I would call
any of this miraculous, or cursed, damned, or whatever
scripture's buzzwords—whether you should or
can dam a miracle from what flows around it. I
say nothing, the way in dreams you can't run.
In the morning after we've fucked again, he's got oats going.
His *signature*: maple syrup, banana, gojis, raisins.
We're quoting *The Simpsons* and giggling.
He asks if I've seen that Mormon show.
He binged it last week. He tells me Jeb's crisis
of faith disturbed him more than the slayings.
I have seen it. I have seen it and it
fucked my relationship to my community forever.
It comes out raw, but I'm okay. He sucks the vape I'll
smell on my clothes long after I've washed them and rained
eucalyptus-oil spray on them. The swollen
raisins taste of ash. Rushing to the shower
I notice on the bottom of the pot a suede of oats so thick
and black, there's no cleaning it.

Log

7am. Day 7.

Drain 1: 24ml, rosé.

Drain 2: 16ml, rosé

Drain 3: 23ml, rosé

Drain 4: 14ml, creek water

Meteor Showers

She takes the sheepskin outside and beats it. Wrecked pottery wheel on the deck windmilling in that way wind has of turning scenes barren. Feijoas crying for water like young for algorithms. Pumpkin vines round the yard aging towards each mirror like egg towards egg in a poaching whirlpool. She slakes the feijoas, pelt slung over her right shoulder because she is her toddler self. If she blinks hard enough sensation will sing again in her chest, her areolae. How he lay on his back on her belly yesterday and confessed: did she remember the song at the good Eltham fruiterer last week? The nothing song? The song they agreed was the flattest, least catchy husk of pop ever pushed out, the musical sibling of the tasteless red apricots they stole, bit, lobbed onto the train tracks? That song has visited him most days since he first heard it as a child. Often, it's there all day. It's his ambience. His silence. It's embarrassing. Does she have a song like that? Only milk and wool song, mother song she ignored; only the song of a potter receiving clay as a sky receives meteor showers, flares of new substance they work, skylike, into the old cup, whose size and shape never alters. When he hears cold leave her. When they loofah each other's cracked necks. When he gauzed his brother's scissor wounds dreaming. When his brother dream-sang. When the flame of her nausea and pain meds flickers. When she vices braids or pressures shut envelopes in the firelight.

Maples

There's this belief (common)
that you can harness
someone to a bed and label this
life life.

There is searching for neat frames of reference like a child for sharp
rocks to draw pictures on larger rocks, and there's a child
finding such rocks

at times when they do not want to draw,
want to crush the rocks, the dust
cloudy as clear liquid

that's entered a glass too hard and too fast. And tenderness
spectra to parse, heat maples to tap. Light

-roast coffees to brew through a sock
Costa Rican-style like he likes, the boy after the depot
injection gone wrong, falling

asleep on his feet, pacing, asleep, rec-yard pacing. There
are drugs. Sharks of rest, sharks of unrest
to lure to a

war for innateness
with a liver as burley. There's life spreading

falsehoods to preserve itself.
Every night words lose
value like bread and every morning
there's bread.

Prepubescence, Warnambool

Near the whaling museum
I watch a woman body
a propane tank onto a Hilux. *More*
Than Propane across the tank.
In the caravan annex sweet

-hot with canvas and grass, Terrence's mum
dollops Flora, yellow as the grass
on packed-up sites, onto bread
that never stales. *Balinese,* she said

yesterday when she spun. Sheer harem pants. Black
bathers so near I caught
neoprene fumes as if I'd hidden in Jetty Surf.
My kind hosts. Each kindness
they lavish on me I salivate, forced to

look at a body not supposed to gape there.
I'm dancing on the breakwater.
On the bluestone parapet. Orphaned. Brotherless. Night sky an X-ray, glare a silver
dye in my lymphatic fluid, her taste in squid ink, wind

stockman hired to corral me
pulling every ploy. The net for wants,
needs, I cast I slit. Lusts. All coast through.
Alone in the fuel. Terrence and I breaststroke to Penguin Island, roofs
of our mouths doughnut-jam-cauterised.

My best friend Terrence
jumps first. I make him
fade and I follow, fairy pairs couples
from the videos under his trundle.

Prolepsis

Now we're old people, we know death
is the price of wisdom. Another way
to word this—*spill blood*

and reap has always been the gods' edict. Remember
Federer, sacrificing boys on green altars?

We've gone the distance. We've held
our blood like that cockatoo between stringybarks
holds its crest's resemblance

to the yellow wildflowers in its belly. The Mountain
Blast Powerade you washed down
pills with in a public bathhouse long ago

tomorrow. The old people who found you told you to wake up
to keep dreaming. The slackness
in the concept of their skin, like spring

lamb resting after a long cooking. Those missions to release
your blood's rescued eagles always false
flags, red carpets

to the next premiere, next altar—that is, most
who want to die die. Most who do not want to die live

longer, perhaps long and lucky
enough to become what we are, what we have
to impart to each other and the rain.

High Tide

You hate fishing. Your denials—their polish-toil alloy—appear.
You hate people. You won't sit with the boy on the pier.

Sand can't forget, the tendons it buries can't. Though the old
coherence becomes new pipis sun-embroidered to the pier.

The first catastrophe is beauty. A bleeding seal pup, accidental
burley. Bull sharks, taunting channel buoys near the pier.

Pier sleepers black with squid ink. Black around the vogue cores,
black around testimonies and suns. Lies lure-adroit on the pier.

Twice a day the tide resents the palaces, the citadel mockeries
that lowered it. The catch grows wary, savvy, coy, and voids the pier.

Hatred is fear. Fear isn't hatred. Fear of death may be hatred
of the self who would be homely and absurd to Him, light's ploy on the pier.

Fishermen toss puffers on the pier road. Traffic wafers them.
Unpeel the wafers, toss them back, hear waking noise from the pier.

That they might stroll together down a road to the local shops
erasing all they passed. That a boy might toy with living on a pier.

God, it's not true. People-lover, you name him Anders: *man, manly.*
Who hates more than men? Whose lines decoy this pier?

Salt and Sea

Old man, how you've transformed.
How the wattle outside your bedroom was
content for thirty years as ornament
and, one night, choked your wife in her sleep
so you uprooted it. You've done it before.
Nightmares of live-export ships. Red cattle. You waking
having eaten your last animal. Old man, be proud.
Picture the little boy, not yet white, rigging the orchard
traps, wringing pigeon necks with hands
within his brother's hands. A twitching
softness, a mercy, as the boy holds
a pencil, a fork, *baccalà* in his mouth, a Bible.
Do you believe, old man, that you can be gentler
than your deeds until your deeds become gentle,
set an example as you betray it, make a cushion
fort for it? You spoke of an armoured
boy beholding a Lord who wouldn't save his father as radiant
sham, a hospital bed's harsh tube lighting.
Such a simple transformation. Simple emptying.
Simple upending. Old man, your mother passed
unable to pronounce your sons' names: *Adenino,*
Andersino, spitting *nespola* pits into an earthenware bowl.
The stillborn she passed. Your few seconds
of little brother when your siblings were grown, and you were not
yet white, and your father was still browning
Earth's wharves. Whether a baby brother
in every closeness cools after his first
breath warms and wets your eyelids. Whether, old man,
you'll tell me his name, or the muteness of which
mausoleum it's engraved in. I'm sorry
for the father at tennis who thinks your son has cheated his
and says, *Look what you raised,* and says, sotto

voce, *Fucking wogs.* Check the mark. Maybe I did cheat.
Maybe I knew I'd get away with it because, unlike you,
I arrived with impunity's pallor. Normal
is seeing someone by not seeing them.
Other is seeing someone by not seeing them. Is there
anything to see there, old man? Is there a transformation
to log? How the young man, *inamorata,* watched
in Abyssinia as, to the glory of Mussolini, his best
friend's body metamorphosed
into meat for the street dogs. How the research scientist dreamt of
cats clawing lab chrome, eyes in speculums
brimful and dilated with whatever funded
theory his dropper held. Every fragment
of meat the man ate smelled of those cats he patted
and sedated—and his father's blank
tornadoes?—and every fragment
wasn't meat at all, loopy as it sounds, was pre- or post
-cruelty the way you taught me primary colours
can't stem from other colours, but are origins
there's no circling back to, though the poet who writes
of salt that can never be sea again fails
—or declines—to mention it never can't be. You subscribe
to *Skeptic* magazine. You've lived a long, Godless life.
Ignore me blathering about primary colours and origins.
Old man, it's halftime: I nest on your lap, whisk
your leg hair into cacti Lego cowboys lasso
and blast Indians around. You make it a fair fight—
give the Indians lightsabers. Spaceships. *Fair to the point*
of unfairness to himself—how do you say that in Italian?
That would make a fine epitaph,
that poor, honourable life instruction. That
might be the first time I've criticised you
which means this is working, this
is loving. A high school, beside Pentridge
supermax prison. Escapees breaking for Merri Creek
locking down freaked, rapt classrooms. Skips

bashing wogs. Wogs and skips bludgeoning
creek snakes with train rocks. Unfathomable:
building a school prison-adjacent—a *never again* like privacy
between priest and altar boy, or my eyes unseeing
you clenching and unclenching
your arse cheeks to Bocelli Christmas songs,
or the smell of Pinetarsol
and your smell not being your smell, old,
white man, who once thought clouds couldn't glow purple as jacaranda bloom.
Once, a boy secreted brains, sweetbreads, *baccalà*
into his shorts pockets, which he inverted
over the outhouse bowl—tongues pronouncing
crudities about freedom. A man ripped open
his hands freeing his boy's yabby lines from rushes
that looked soft, but were razors. I'm warning you
that *Andersino*, what your mother called me,
is almost *Anderssein*, what Hegel called the escapee
in us, the other who answers
to *death* or *child*. Old man, old shapeshifter, now I'm old
as you were when you conceived me
you are going—I'm waiting, I'm
escaping, I've crossed the creek and I'm numb and running
—to show me how to love you, how to suffer
love, transform ornament
into bloom so potent it's an enemy.

Before the Burglary

The boys' father is hitting them
balls at the YMCA.

In your room, to Sting, you shimmy
out of the moss-green

Versace pantsuit you bought on lay-by on consignment.
From your dresser's bottom drawer, you remove the sewing box.

Pincushions. Grandmother's jewellery.
Upon the fields of barley. Costume junk, mostly.

You heap it on the bed. You wear everything.
Gloves of rings. Bangle gauntlets. Lockets, beads, pearl necklaces

festooning your head and ears, like Christmas lights.
As we walk through fields of gold. Goodbye,

beetles floodlight-drunk, slurried
beneath the boys' feet. Goodbye, suit guilt.

Aftercare

Spell the word correctly and nothing happens.
Spell the word wrong and the quiz
-master chooses a whip off the rack and lashes you.

Imagine your threshold, your reef
break, as a wading pool, and those coral
cuts I'm going to inflict the simple
conversion of your whole being into opium.

Imagine helium balloons so high they're red nicks in the clouds.
I don't want more Tempranillo. I'm over talking
about veterinary school, that was small talk. Treading.

You know what happened at the dog shelter, what they made me do there.
That you're all head is making it hard
for me to be all whip. *Supercilious. Pusillanimous.*

So it took you three tries to spell *embarrassed* in grade three.
This is not where you punish or exult—or punish

-exult—that child. You're a bright boy. You think that
gets me off—being a vector for self-hate?
Am I human?

Get dressed. They're waiting: your reefs of language. Your
warrens, hermitages, marrow atolls, hearts

of palm. You're not the first to leave like this.
Black, instead of black and blue.
Confused about what I offer. Aftercare. *A-f-t-e-r.*

Boulevards

Peak hour. You're headed west
into dusk's verbenas and their bladder
will bloom if you don't exit here,

take the park road until it's seabed
-corrugated, single-lane, unlit track to the river,

to the lot and toilet block there.
How simple. Almost regal. You must
pretend to get over, while you bury

the betrayal in your breath for how they've torched that road. That night
from which, since you were small, every time you've passed it, you've barred yourself.

You must guard the other places. Boulevards
of do-not-enter. Start now—hold them
nowhere except as resolve's blue pulse. You must be ancient
Nonna Tina with her topaz cross, tangelo juice

beading from whiskers onto a mandolin
strung with blessed horse gut. God

knows it's spoilt survival. Control—its river
border with abandon. Subjection. Verbena. That trust must vacate
before the wind rusts. That the house in childhood burning to white frame

must burn on if you're to be free: yes, laws
rust; no, pedantry isn't rule.

It's exile. In an alley, they find
relief. Find yours. Rest. Rejoice—touch
warm body, high and low.

Spa

Jets not inhaling, not exhaling
—a belt of mute chrome.

Front-beach sand at the filter mouth.
If you wanted to gather

the sand for analysis, you could know
with what poultice of

deep time you dab your limbs
raw, kind. If you wanted

to know the sacred you could towel off and know the sacred.
If you wanted to sleep naked in this heat

of backstep, declare it not real
and false—concaved

breath, revenants—but real and true,
substantiated, intrinsic, you could come

home from effort's misadventures
to soak and soften in bliss.

Around the World

For a limited time, anyone
who buys a K-Mart basketball hoop
gets a cut-out of Shaq. Life-size.
Michael puts his in his room. Shoulders
broad as wedge-tail wings. The hoop
goes in the driveway with water
weighting the base, stablising it.
Michael and the neighbour play Around the World.
Often from his bedroom, Michael sees
the neighbour up that tree with the sour orange
fruit more pit than fruit, staring at the sky. One evening
Michael's too sick for footy training
so his mum goes to the shops instead.
Soon as her car leaves, the neighbour comes
and does something that leaves
Michael basketball-fleshed after he
and the neighbour have gone
to different high schools and fallen
out over a sweetheart and grown
to hate each other officially. He watches
it happen—the neighbour taps all his force
to rattle the hoop base so water
darkens the driveway concrete, which must exhale
heat—it's a hot autumn—as if the eagle
Michael's uncle poisoned and stuffed just
hatched there, thrashed-Sega-cartridge heat;
and each time the neighbour licks
the dark spill he holds
his shoulders, his biceps, his belly, listening for Michael
can't guess what. How long until Michael discovers
Shaq's gaze on him? Mouthwaters at
salt on skin game-slick?

Sunday Morning Near Yea

Through paddock mist, he watches me
buckle complicated shoes. Is he laughing
at the fire siren or is the siren his
ex's surgical drains, or his Nonno in that circus, 1920's,

right-angled on Roman rings, clown wig askew?
Stolen-copper light. Migraine's bathwater
that boils your skin if you swirl it.
Soon, we'll have appointments, lose each other to some

drives or redactions. Soon—I've seen him—he'll more openly mine the silver
hairs from his chest and eat them. They'll taste like fire—
big dogs over a road will
sound like oil leaping from bark on fire.
It'll be null in my unit. For warmth, I'll redline

my laptop on my belly. Licking the screen
will be images of which I'm so ashamed
I'll belong to a hundred families, a nebulised
dark-web IP. Even when you don't care for one another, when you're after
an eager body, you need common

ground and the ground often is shame. I don't make the rules.
What fire will his shame ban this bright sobering?
Will he too, once he's alone—he will: look at him—indulge
the presumption of the illicit?

The presumption that the light's copper is stolen.

Cattle low. Calves. The party smoulders. I have him
craze my eyebrows with his fingers
and, with my weed scissors, edge them.

Override: Nocturne

Feet never having warmed, I'm live.
Cloud below the moon, black
coals below a spit lamb. My vision steams
when piss fills the Aladdin
thermos on my desk for this. Still wet,

sudsy—the lambskin I bought last week at the market lilac
with the fur of what dreamt on it. Night
says to wring it onto the carpet, lay it on the oil heater.
Says to lick loose fleece from my palms, burn

moonlight's remains waxing
a jacket in the garage; I do, until every seam
bathes cured, until brute
thirst to task the sponge grips the sponge.

Is the sleepwalker sleep's
crisis or miracle? Below tube fluorescents, I'm gnashing
gauze off a reel. Hydrogen
peroxide still rivers
the medicine-drawer base, warps it. His open

arms, in coils of white pile, soft
as the lambskin he wet and suckled as a baby.
But it's distant—his head as I hold it to dress him,
like mushroom cloud on old film. So lavender
oil does override. Peace does split air. Inside, tiger

brindle sears into the pelt where the element hits. It will stiffen, then crack, as in
be tended. Picture the thermos steel's silver.
Smell and taste the colour silver. River
nitrogen. Taste my brother's skin.

Game Day, Post-Op

Time to debut a body that's yours
as a camel is a rider's. You take a dusk
jog, cut through Lincoln Park Zoo, polar bear's
laps and laps across glass a pacesetter.

On the lakeshore trail, you find your favourite mile
gone. Climate change. The unruliness
of what swells. While you lay in bed, wounds draining, tissue
expanders leavening with fluid, the curve where you flowed
emptiest broke for the depths. In its stead is this
fenced sandbagged zone construction

lights eerie. A vessel's maiden voyage. Hull
with the lights' glass granuling over it. Camel again. Waterfall
brushed from the dark
hollow behind a waterfall. You and he
—if he stays; if you can bear that—will have to work
this numbness lest it scar
as the scars scar. Unfitness is your breath

oxidising you. You debuted a body
when you were five or six at a wedding, rose
for a bride who was the perfect
error—her identical twin, a bridesmaid. Zoo body a cathedral
of gaze ran through, made falling
just short the effrontery at its core. Time to spot

the debutant over temporary fencing. No feeling, no feeling
your life again in the old fix when the lake bucked
rain onto Wrigley Field on game day. Sink
the base path in gasoline. Scorch it primed.

Promiscuity

Dawn. The eggshell walls blush. Open
mouths under torchlight. I'm a tongue, what else?

Forgetting how to pronounce
your mouth, its tartness, the morning

after drugs and mango and black sapote. How to answer jaw
pressure that whispers, *Nest here.*

Let go. How to say bondage
is liberty's nearest and most camera-shy moon.

I light the Coonara. Lolly wrappers burn green. O, freedoms
that strip the lungs. Hunger ageless. Flamingoes
stained their hunger's dawn blush.

You couldn't look at me between your legs without rubbing
your carer's crown under ward fluorescents.

We hauled what they cut from you, woke yoked
together in the egg

of what your rips wept. Going to pieces—powerlessness—is erotic.
Staying in pieces is lessness.

Forgetting how to say, *Slowing*, and mean *Savouring*.
Lovers break up to see what they have.

A tongue detaches to see speech. It sees silence and nothing
thrills it more. Nothing renews it more.

Moving Day

Come, mate, step off Elgin Street
and into the river
house, the cliff place on stilts, locals

call it the castle, far above the water,
far enough to lose the water
texture, smooth it, shark cartilage, the smoothness

of the boy's slick arms and lychee
footpads two decades
back on the tennis court, on the road side of the net

hemming texture from smoothness—
come in from this Friday
frost, it's brisk, from freezing

me with my name, the surname's i's and l's
in order, come in from there, Mr.
Memory, from the bars you're set to open, the tens

of thousands you banked tuning
supermarket fridges, pandemic money, so much
it was nothing, a smooth sum, from

nothing back to nothing—come
gather your things
from the rooming house, I'll wait here, lay

them out here in your new rumpus room
on its floorboard gloss in its
smooth river vista under its cornices, as its skin

-pricking light off the water—come, invite
me in, I am the fact
of the kid, quiet, gaze light

scraps jagging earthward, fair-to-poor
timer of the yellow ball, polo shirt, hair that beard's
taupe, straight, smooth, no product,

no texture, I've got to run
to work, leave him with you, possum
rain across your new roof the musk

of river breathing and dreaming at night, come back
down after the morning's
twelve espressos

and four amber ales, yeasty
river on your black paint-flecked down jacket,
come all, come one,

ask about America, boiling
water and dumping it
from a stock pot off a balcony and watching

waterfall freeze in flight, ask
how much wool to wrap around yourself
in your new bed before the weight

retracts the warmth, no more me,
come back from that security
contract in Port Moresby without those

screws loose, your castle
awaits you—redgum letterbox, bread-warm
-empty-house loneliness, dogs

and baths needing running—come across
the border loose, no panicked
ankle bracelet, no smooth bald patch—come away from him

in the pub the treefall
of him against that woman's eye socket his
pumped coarse chest splitting

window glass like water, making light
of surface tension, come
now, come now, come to, bury your

fingers in your golden retriever's smooth
copper coat, not the man's
windpipe to resuscitate him

so he sees you her hero
punish him more, sees without texture, river
gazing up as cloud lands on it, soft

numb lesson, koan, two children, come, you're
home, Jake, yes, that's your name
on the deed, the evergreens

in your new yard are showering
dew along the radiance
of your name

Wish

Do something for me, lover,
brother, whomever's

lamp this rubs. Go to the state park
where we saw the lovemaking

lorikeets and looked away.
Go to this clearing, stand there.

As you shift the air
in your knuckles, say, *These are his*

biases. Unearth blue-hooded
mushrooms and eat them.

Watch, in the sun's zenith,
me at my outdoor table eating a sandwich,

my cat in oxalis nearby, playing
dead as a lorikeet nears.

Look around this thought:
Kill the bird, and it will be my fault.

When the teeth pulverising bread
freeze, when the throat forgets how to swallow,

in proof's stillness, dance,
crack again.

Poison

Our father, naked on the bed's long edge, calls
the shorebird formation over Cape Schanck

at sunrise a fire-ant trail. At one end, cloud
fruit, a *nespol*a from our old tree, jammy
and breathing; at one end, the nest. His

hamstrings oily as if with lanolin. Bedspring creak and the
crinkle of him biting black

cotton underwear from its wrapper. None of these sounds
bells. Bedside food scraps and medical books.

Our father spits staples into the shag. They vanish.
Would a good son recover them? Would a good son
urge him not to dress after what you did in visiting hours,

not to raise the venetians? How forcing sky
into flesh risks breaking it—the flesh, the sky.

God's been whispering to you in a child's voice. Like all children
raised in a house without God, maybe we were
the lucky ones—raised in a house where God stood

a chance of being truly infinite. Or this just vacant
prayer for you. Like the storm-scent of loom-fresh cotton. Like the violet
night, weeks before they auctioned the house,

when our father went to the back shed for nails
and saw the *nespola* tree breathing. Glinting. You've
heard this one. Orion's Belt in the torch beam. The eyes

of thousands upon thousands of rats. The bells
    of our father's breath digesting

that what happened next would be barbaric, like the remoteness
    of telling you not to come home.

Udders

Try to remember: it's the word
remember rattling
your mind's windowpanes
like a cattle truck. Try to forget and
same thing, only your mind

is the truck and the object
of forgetting the windowpanes, the flimsy
apartment they exhibit
inside which lie two teenage boys in a bed.
They're post-party drunk.

In the night, one of the boys will wake
to an unlocatable feeling
as if he were concrete
floor someone sweeps with a stiff broom.

As his being's rooms lighten
the boy will realise that his friend is caressing him,
rubbing fledgling beard against his face,
milking the udders of his hair.

Yes, the caresser is dreaming
of the girl who broke up with him a few days ago—in the dream
world, that is who the caressed is

and in the waking world
also, which is to say the boundary
has undressed and they lie here. One
can only hold
open a portal a few ways.

Callery Pears and Blue Hatches

Near close, a parking garage
silos you with your footsteps, gaunt
aural shadows.
Your car, a blue hatch, won't show itself.
Escape hatch. Shows itself

in what it's not—blue sedans; your fingers
in a bookstore up the jacket
back of your father to the coccyx
fluff of a stranger, your scream, then the soap

smell and squish of your father
stranger—that that in the
this that breath hitches at. From the street
the Callery pear finds you. You saw it coming in.

Smelled it. The *come tree,* in blossom. Every storey. When you lost
your family forever
at the surf beach, you'd have drowned
the red-haired boy in the parking lot for his place
and name—could the boy's

parents have homed, adored their error?—in that minivan.
The right to the ramps' mass. The pear scent's must
-escape-the-scent; what in the scent is the first
pleasure and first pain dealmaking.

To offramp from the always-both.
Blue hatch again: yours, yours, not yours.
Is there just one? That knot
through breath's sail when it was yours
is yours.

Cats

I must know the future. I'm going to live it exactly as it happens.
    It happens every time I close my eyes: a fuchsia rhombus, afloat.

Afloat on envy's lagoon, I find the house rearranged and added to.
    Added to the kitchen is a jade cheeseboard on a nail over the sink.

Over the sink, the cheeseboard sways in a draught with no source.
    No source as in the nonworld of what I neither effect nor witness.

I do not witness my housemates adding and rearranging.
    I do not effect the metamorphosis from rhombus to magic carpet.

Carpet burns tiger your legs when we fuck in the portable classroom.
    When we'll fuck in the portable classroom, I know the future

grows by contracting, dozes orgasmic through every beginning.
    In the beginning who kissed cats and threw them across the yard?

Across the yard, the *nespola* tree leaks jade milk from axe wounds, leaks bees.
    Bees lagoon beneath my carpet, flight it into the future.

The future where my handprints don't recede from your surface.
    Your surface the rhombus. Chessboard. Nonworld mammoths roam.

Coconut Crab

At the market it was scuttling between taro and yams like legs of beef. Vines bound its pincers. Under the thatched roof, on the concrete slab, it was free, trusses and price tag aside. I followed it. Crouching as if I were one, like at the toboggan park when you wore pants the run-chrome grey, or when yabbying we tied chuck steak to our hand-reel lines and zinged it to our tongues in a show of solidarity to exploit. When I wrote *scuttling*, I could have written nothing else. Bagpipes skirl. Bublé croons. These are medicine. These brothers. Slowing myself to stay behind it made me think of Xeno and the dignity in doing something poorly a long time. Persistence without improvement. Dad jazzing up the yard by painting mesh outdoor chairs orange. Me chasing anger, empathy. Art. It led us to hands of plantains I wished would hold me as a ship's bow holds a heron as on the horizon flying fish erupt. It led us under tables to fresh-pulped kava, machetes, tourists waxing cannibalism and the Prince Philip cult. It led us to a divination stall. I'd never seen a psychic. Never had my tarot read. I did write that poem about her about oracle bones, portents in bone-cracks of this or that cosmic event, often solar, often eschatological. I did ask her love and your healing of a freak white eyelash. I bought a question. I'm not sure the diviner understood English. But their smile, as the candle leapt from lit to unlit, had a taste. A fruit. Like its sweet flesh when it led us—all visions do—to the place where it boiled.

Come to the Circus

more chest hairs lose pigment

at five and three-quarters

in a play he played

a circus owner

red blazer gold epaulettes

tall anita was his daughter

laura may

daddy the show must go on it must

Calm Voice

On a fatherhood weekend, the men drag
a dead manna gum, chained to a ute, into camp.
They're talking innocence. Is it inborn, or clad
layer by layer by behaviour? Around the grey stump
the men start chainsaws and crack beers, open
a phone (there's reception), search *innocence definition.*
Blamelessness. Chastity. Childhood. But also
integrity, which means innocence. The confusion
—that integrity means wholeness too—
heats up when one man says he heard children
arrive with sin. Then two-stroke fumes
drown the twilight bush's scat-and-pepper scents.
They cut it. Some of the men scream, some don't,
when spiders erupt from the warm hollow.

When spiders erupt from the warm hollow
a man tells a story. Halfway down a hill
between three brothers' house and the park where ghosts
shoot up in the centre of the oval
there's a house, double-block, yellow brick.
It's for orphaned and homeless youths. At night
—any night—twenty kids sleep there. No strict
rules can stop it from sounding like a hundred, like
a Slipknot concert. The exiles find new shadows.
The men roll the logs into the last campers' pit.
Twice in the brothers' childhood, the house goes
up in flames. Cops comb its yard for knives. For bits
of evidence because these kids are bad.
They steal one brother's Razor scooter. They're bad.

They steal one brother's Razor scooter. They're bad
thieves—the two younger brothers see them
from their bedroom, tell their older brother, who's had
enough and leads them down. Twigs, kerosene,
and three 18V leaf blowers and it's blazing,
a mountain range whose peaks scratch the dark sky
of gum canopy and dark sky. They sedate him
with words, calm voices, or try, the carers: *why*
risk arrest over this? The man recalls
the woman saying, *I'm speaking in a calm voice.*
Chanting it. A spell. But there are walls
she bruises then, backing inside. Her voice
like the TV cabinet glass he puts
her through. The boy from a good home. Voids her.

What did the boys from a good home lose, shed, void
that day? Not the older brother, but the
ones on the street who summoned him. The boys
who saw a woman valued less than a scooter
at an age when the worth of things was molten
glass for heroes to blow. It's the world,
one man says. This fire's the world and when
the fireworks go off later, it'll be all
our evolution reaching its end point—
bright lights and explosions. Ginger steeps
in cast iron, drugs strike blood, charcoal anoints
a lentil stew, which dissolves the man's story.
Talk moves on. A herd eating sweeter grass.
One man's dog pulls a roo bone from the ash.

One man's dog pulls a roo bone from the ash
and it turns to spiders, which turn to ash
on the younger brother's eyelids, to ash
in the middle brother's memory settling

when the younger brother comes, asks, *Remember*
when you led us down the hill to find the kid
who'd thrown a hot dog at me? Remember
kicking his door till he answered, joined
in calling himself what you called him, licked
my shoes? The middle brother had forgotten
himself back to an innocence the quick
of which is fire, innate combustion.
Around the fire, the men talk skin-to-skin
touch in the early months, so love burns in.

Errand

They're pulling a green wagon full of green waste
down a green-winged dirt road. They may be
going to the council compost centre, all of them
—he, his brothers, his wife, the smog
-red sun, the lollipop man from primary school with his high-vis and open
palm that could halt a drunk or livestock truck, laughing
deer tacky with tamarack resin, his wife's guitar teacher,

the Wife of Bath, *without a shirt*
boy in Paul Jennings, Narcissus, Narcissus's alien reflection,
oxen—all of them pulling their weight, harmonising
or synchronised-swimming, road and bush the body
and wings of a dragon with a helpless human
child's face which is the sky ahead and the place where their whole surplus
heap meets its mulcher, churns

to a worm butter of leaves and frond and leaves
and fronds as which it will reharden,
resoften. Then, at random, his little brother
drops his share. The wagon lists with a steam-train
derailment's panache, its baroque. In his wife's voice, his little brother
says he is very sick—how many green
years can he waste here on this straight in this pooled errand?

He has to braise ox tongue, eat punnets of world
-record-sized blueberries
in fistfuls, win fat on the greyhounds, pulp faces like watermelons,
pump EDM as he dances atop police cars. Don't the others realise?
This is too much. Too fast. To slow it down you have to
speed it up beyond speed. His brother says this
as a crackling, from callistemon lips.

Swede

It has stopped raining and the forest—who would call it a forest—is raining. You're running your circuit. Roads. Shopfronts. Factories. Roads. A cornrowed child, face a red-jam symphony, holds out a pinwheel as you pass them. *Whirligig*, Dad called it when he won your brother one in a Royal Show strength game. You are your parents' age when they imagined you. In China, pinwheels represent fortunes turning. At the rubbish bag of empty cat-food cans beneath a factory stoop, you slow. None today. Once, you saw four—two calicos, a tabby, and a black slip with one green and one blue iris. Collarless. Bones and skin folds. Never eating. Through the roller door, rows of twelve-volt batteries charge like lab livers. How your brother would retch when he saw Mum washing cat-food cans in the dishwater. The tabby grey of this murk. Your theory has been that a person feeds the cats, apple in possum hollows, white bread for ducks, pigeon seed. That this litter might have wound up in a laundry sack like in Dad's nightmares of train rocks and pond. See it now: pinwheels as torture wheels. Someone planted these cans. The cats had to find them. Constellate for them. The cats have forsaken hunts for this scent. Muzzles red from can rims. The cats can't leave. The cats will starve here. Like a Swede, you're running with the bag, thinking of him calling from prison, thinking until you cry of running through the rain and returning it.

Heir

The one, the many
beneath this one, waiting

to show your life the tolerance
of dissent. They're near. The hearth

mussed. A burnt-out
waiting to be despotic when lovers
want this. Tomorrow, when you

flick-knife your armpit hair, scatter it in public
toilets, scan these pooled

arabesques, don't tell me you can't divine
the rebellion

in keratin as the latch trembles. Don't tell me the oily
breaths in the air vent aren't arias

at an empty auditorium's windows, heat
verses rippling the panes.

Don't tell me you can't feel the radiance
of opening up—that this wouldn't

be a swinging open of the promise held
gaze holds, an anchorite's cell

cramped as a moon. Patient,
mouth in mirror, their waiting

is their frailty. Your terror
their want or accession.

Log

10pm. Day 14.

Drain 1: 14ml, creek water

Drain 2: 10ml, bird bath

Drain 3: 15ml, bird bath

Drain 4: sand dune

Hymns

That light sweeps across Blue Lake
    like shadow reminds me that the inverse is
always shadow; brings me to your hands
changing, changing, changing,

            changing the flow of velvet grain. We were
            piss-sword-fighting, the moment we saw our first
            snake with breath in it. Not rotten, not tyre-streaked. A tiger molten
            as the birth of the boulder it sunned on.

Blue Lake was a quarry, remember? That black
    coil reminds me of drinking from hot garden hose.
Vinyl's taste, feel on the palate, like ink,
a pen leak, brings me to the stick

                    -and-poke tattoos on your arms growing
                    more venomous, as if the skin were rotting. Because
                    the skin is rotting, I think of the men
                    up and down our road in childhood, caving in

curbside lindens, corridoring them,
    for powerlines. That it was the only way through
takes me to me to your big brothers
warning you to pull that

                    thumb out of your gob, toss Blankie into Blue Lake
              or else. You could barely walk, which reminds me of our young
          cousin's funeral mass. The blistered red
leather hassocks. The father's sermon

against *woo-woo spirituality.* His praise
    shadowed by defensiveness, hubris, self
-conversion, brings me to hymns I sing too late of
you as safe and good, Hosanna.

Athabasca

across the glacier
to a clean slit in the ice
blade through white fish
the guide crouches
a small child at the brook lip
take off your mittens
drink this and your hair
will turn white
your soul will turn pure
white water white
icescape white thought
child becoming ice
and shattering an elk
calf onto birth
-staggered legs
adult popping
white hairs from a chest
sucking the cool
white bulbs free
what if they were wrong
what if truth is heat
not white heat
horseshoeing into cold
the heat of spring puddles
spawn heat
not even heat
not even truth
what then would this ice
cube at your lips bid you
let go a child's balloon
into shadeless sky

Collecting Brown Matter in Lockdown as the Climate Warms

This was at the outset of adorable years
The earth loved us a little I remember.
—René Char, 'Évadné,' translated by Mary Ann Caws

When the rain lets up, we drive around, pulling over here
and there to stuff linden leaves in black bags.
It's not a competition to see who can fill theirs fastest, or who can file
their nails on the kerb the most fabulously, or whom the escaped

centipedes in the car will favour.
It's just you and me driving in circles on the brink
of our given radius. A moon of compliance, at apogee. We're
heating the cigarette lighter. Why are we heating the cigarette lighter?

For the same reason your skin is the colour of a leaf
I can't imagine. The mycelial networks in the soil you call
to. Call empires. The glacial in your smell. The ships of camels I dream of
turning back before they run aground and become culls.

Creeks run around rocks, root boles. Can't we speak around viruses?
The '90s: Crocodile Mile—dish-soaped tarp on the lawn, the open
jaws bellied through at splashdown; leaded fuel; AU Falcons; *Rage*
not airing clips with lingerie-clad bodies, or death themes.

How afternoon hogged the ball then.
Driving around, we pass a girl standing across the street
from a house I bet is her own, from parents I bet are waiting for her
to slink into punishment's earshot. We pass her again: the way she secrets

both hips behind a plane tree with dagger leaves and just peers, as if
ownership were lamplight yet to fill a room. As if the cigarette lighter
were a planet, ringed by sun, cooling in our hands. Let's agree
we've been this girl to each other. Let's decide whether to brand each other

is to caress. Glitter under our nails, we stuff plane leaves in black bags,
drive around. Around and around. Do you get the sense we've run
this script figureless times? Are centipedes wild lips? Maybe forgetting is
impossible after all, and this is the old springtime.

When Closing Jackson-Pratt Drains

Squeeze out air for best suction. Steadiness
the pain barrier. Ignore the purple
in the dawn light that is not at

all purple; pay the envy in
the sparrow in the bird bath thin mind.
Like too-raw sunlight, site bruising

will float across vision as a gentle
prismatic havoc. Retape and unkink

tubing, re-pin to nightdress. Tighten the stopper.
Check the suture. Press in clean fingers
of the eyes the urge

to rebuke the sun, the sparrow—blame
the pain barrier
and bearer. Sop spills. Gentler.

Gentlest. Have patient name the far-off melody
the old sleeping
dog wheezes. Distract, but quell

laughter. Have woozy patient re-gloss
a silvered deck or cut

bangs and flower stems in the same handful
at the same jag. Duet
rakes through diaphragm gravel.

Helium

In ways, you already know how
long the vase will stay in pieces.
You know helium can float a person
out of the world. What changes
then? Is it that the Amazon
of summer air on the lungs
augments knowing? Is it alacrity
after torpor? What is knowing
they might lock you up—what is rumbling
into bed cycloned in that?
Do you cherish or resent your freedom?
What is it, anymore, freedom?
Are your dreams ever not wrung? Oh yes, here
comes an old move: holding suffering
as sacred when of course it is(n't). Of course
your face in pieces opens
a pelican bill at the boat ramp, distends it
with guilt's offal. Of course I loathe what you've done.
Menace. Pariah. Lyrebird.
You know, in ways, to condemn yourself.
As you are, baby brother,
yourself, I can offer no love, no dignity
rounder than condemnation. Boys again: the tense, rubbery
seaweed berries we toil in Woolamai
surf all summer trying to split, to pop,
wave legions we try to cow
but can't. They're too tough. Mythic
defiance of onslaught. Once, someone heard
human resilience had no limit
at a time when this lesson was a sacrament
and not the mother dread.
The life you carry says it too, without

cease, without equivocation,
because it's a sun. Not a waxen
paper bag plump with gas. A sun.

Hammer

tell your students the trick
                to writing well is to take your subject
        so seriously

hammer the puck
                of your subject
        harder so hard it strikes

a bell and a wave
                of carnival prizes
        barrels

Birth

We walked to the beach barefoot
when the sand was warm and the sun not

far beneath the horizon, as near the waterline as a child
on the bottom bunk to a god atop them.

The tide rose. Wind fed our fires
to death. I wrapped your feet in my shirt hem.

Over that, my hands. Through a crack, mouth
breath hot as a soul could engineer.

Somewhere under there, ruptured pipeline gushing gas into a dark pristineness.
You lay on your back down a dune,
skull to tide, blood-drunk, blood

swale. Later, you likened washing your
feet of their wrapping to birth—

hot, moist, swell. Birth, when we crammed
our bones into the cabin shower, and I couldn't breathe

and suck at the same time. I couldn't agree
or disagree, not having been born. The night

clouds could no longer pipe milk.
I read a cuttlebone in the sand. Rubbed it against my terror, my humour.

South became west. I was long
gone when the cold left you.

Libretti

You spend your welfare payment on a dinner package to the opera. *Madama Butterfly*. You rent a suit, tie, waistcoat, black, black, black, starched white shirt. A man with black hair and white regrowth takes your measurements. He blushes when you ask him to show you how to tie a tie and he has no idea, he hasn't had this job long, not that you'd have known, not that he knows what you've done. *Di rincorrerla furor m'assale, se pure infrangerne dovessi l'ale*. No shoe rentals. You buy a pair, $79.95 on Afterpay. Black loafers, silver *fleur-de-lis* buckles. You leave in character. You're a tenor. From the bag with the clothes and shoes you wore here you smell vanilla vape, drug sweat, coin metal—the funk of a fresh corpse. Your soles slide on the buffed shopping-centre floor like air-hockey pucks. See him, drinking a Coke spider from a clamshell milkshake glass no store here uses? Does he look familiar? Tell him you're off the opera. I can't give you what you're asking for at the station, I'm off to the opera. *Madama Butterfly*. You head downtown, park at the peak of a multistorey. Hot wind soothes from somewhere. *Affonda l'ancora alla ventura*. Your suit's rumpled. Your dinner could be worse. It's French. It needs salt, but you're afraid you'll hurt the waiter. You tip lavishly. For most of the show a mist of incomprehension and perfume drapes, enchants you. You lead the ovation. Near the Shrine, you wade into a pond and become an eel. *Si, tutto in un istante io vedo il fallo mio*. Your mother calls. Your cousin played Pinkerton at La Scala. Renato Cioni. You Google him. There he is, how dramatic, CCTV, your eyes, your suit, attacking a stranger as rush-hour carriages disgorge.

Berries

Rupture is measure. I've lost you—
the story has shape. Let's call it a glass
bauble I'm holding, turning over, searching

for the time I found you
most beautiful. I think I have it. Chicago
snow hushes the streets—sand-dune quiet.

Four post-surgical drains hang from your front.
Full, silicone-tacky, they're the berries
on that Woolamai seaweed I burst

as a kid and drank. Pearled myself in when
the dunes hid my body—my cruelty—and burst. As a bath runs
I squeeze the drains empty, stinging

you a little, a little more. You're faint. Impossible
pink circles on your cheeks—the fireplace
matryoshka dolls your Russian grandpa

gifted you at birth, along with this gene
you're fighting with such beauty. In a Moleskine, I note
time, volume, and colour. Days one

through three, the discharge is iodine
against the sink porcelain, cardinals at the iced window. Who knew
healing's thirst. I read you *Of Wolves and Men* and watch

termites mend their tower post-cyclone.
The flow (the fear) eases. Clarifies—thin,
warm broth. Hot seawater. At bedtime, you melt

on Tramadol into your cushion dunes.
Some nights I wake licking wall. Some nights your hair
smells of iodine. You're twenty-five, on the crest

of beauty's wave and you're an old woman
in a compression bra, wetsuit fabric,
whom an old man nurses as he breathes.

Of Touching

Three days after the mauling
the dog pools at the back of its crate.
It eats and drinks little. With its muzzle
it has balled and swept
its blankets into the corner
it studies, as if needing the comfort
it has renounced to loom. Milk
-white gunk wreaths its eyes.
Tonight, the passerby whose jaw
the dog turned over like earth will gasp
out of surgery. They'll hold
sway in its punishment. Its survival.
For now, the dog lies there.
Surgical cone on its head, forelegs gauzed.
You and your parents having
grown to fear the dog, its crate sits in a spare room
with drawn blinds and a TV pack.
Tonight, pacing the hall, wondering
whether to go in, whether
or when the phone will ring, you hear
the *M*A*S*H* credits, sadder than you remember,
canned laughter—a frozen engine turning over.
After seeing two or three in your life

you've seen three foxes this week, road
fires at mist hours, their hours, a fact
you must ascribe to the dog, a vigour
portent, sovereignty like a new vowel, strands
of saffron through pale dough. Earth
-worms through compost.
Through your pocket, your hand flexes
for the dog's door with foxness.
In the rumpus room, Netflix
tumbleweeds the fifty-inch. The *nespola* tree
smacks the back fence, pulls back, a
strange, many-limbed forging tool, a man
injuring himself, requiring attention
at levels that edge
into needlessness. Into numb
and numbing spectacle. Through the window
the tree's darkness is the dog asleep
in the car boot after a beach day, its dark
fur a mess of spines
so sharp-looking it scared you
to imagine touching them. You've always thought
it a jagged thing.
A noise: your mother jumps. Touches
pulse points. It's just the dog
scratching itself in long, limp strokes.
When it was a pup, you carried it

up the *nespola* tree, a few metres, laid
it in the treehouse on those wool blankets fruit
bats shat all over, and you both dozed.
It fell. As it fell, you were scratching
its name into the trunk and drinking the green
blood its name tapped—drinking yourself
strong on the romance of protecting it. Next
door's roast smells like it's in here.
You pick at your food, go to bed.
Old *nespole* on the kitchen table
bull hide tanning. Still dressed, you
haunt a sofa in your old room where the dog
spent its early life also. That white pen.
All your nightmares and climaxes.
All your vanity, prayers for favour in its thick
bowel-and-shredded-paper air.
It may die tomorrow. The pup you fed
lollies from your mouth
sometimes like a hatchling. The pup
may find itself locked forever in the crate
of death that is living
a boxed life. You are in your primary school's
miniature corridors
kneeling at its miniature urinals
—thinking, that is, of past
scales, ravenous for contraction

and enlargement at once, always
thinking of yourself
as the owl you watched updraft
into a cathedral bell and heard open
its throat—when the crate makes
a broken sound and the spare room opens.
Click-clack of the dog's nails.
It's in the kitchen. Your father follows—
his slipper footsteps, the black
cotton underpants he must wear.
The cheap soap his pores must sweat.
A growl—fang-bearing. Your father
runs back, tells your mother
it has slipped its cone; it's ripping its bandages,
too—you hear this. Your father calls
an all-night vet. There's talk of the pound
until the dog has your parents
screaming in a new, old tone,
running into the rumpus room.
You are there.
You never left the sofa
and you are there. From the kitchen
you see your mother's and father's
heads above the couch hiding them.
They must be crouching strangely;
their knees must know big pressure.

Stay where you are. The dog
destroys its bandages and you watch.
You watch it eat some of the gauze,
gag, raise its hackles at phantoms,
gallop back to its room.
Hulked on blankets. A country
on a sinking atoll. You reach in
through the supple place where the
barking whips its red froth,
where the plaque near the gums shows
dull and mortal.
Clip its leash to its spiked collar.
Come. You know it will. In the laundry
you know what you need
from the first-aid drawer. A bottle
of hydrogen peroxide spills. You know
not to clean it. There are and there are
no intervals between the drips.
Drips doubt and flow yes.
None of this is happening to you.
The house's prime light is at the table.
You lift two empty animals.
Among the *nespole*, downy,
shaved legs, veined
and warm like just-fired rifle barrels—
they weren't sure if the victim

gashed them defending his eyes
or if the dog mauled itself.
You have not touched these legs in years.
You are touching them
dreaming of touching them. You
stanch the blood. Prime with alcohol.
Pools as a tide lopes in slow, the
breaths deepen. While you double
-wrap the gauze, you count
with cotton-wool cadence
from a thousand like your mother
when with a face cloth
in the bath she stroked baby
shampoo from your hair;
you tell it in the dog tongue
in which you have told it things
you have told nobody,
not even yourself,
told it dumb common things,
that it is a good dog, a good boy.
It doesn't react.
You air-kiss its damp muzzle.
The rumpus room is dark.
Your parents have turned off the lights.
Light—that there is; darkness
—that there is more: the two

foods terror eats, a body
eating its own protein and fat;
the two protectors. Keepers. There they are,
traced in the moonlit window,
nespola tree behind them steady
in its mania, mid-fruiting, two heads, two
love silos, two low gods with fluid
and arthritis in their knees
witnessing a game they created
become something else
until it's foreign, the couch back
the cloud they laugh from.

Hottest Day of Summer

white clouds
archipelagic
   the temple's bird baths dry

half-full
with desiccated skinks
   the last

   reaching is for water
inside the beloved
she will not blink she will watch

her fat blood
plum
   become a prune

   and confirm the soul is everything
it has lost
to become what it is

island-hopping
   cabbage moths

she must forgive herself for being sometimes

   unable to forgive
this cruel heat she has
to forgive it

Dinner Call

You're playing *Age of Empires.*
Your settlement, still new, in its dawn, glows
at the bottom of the screen like a starving
Coonara's embers. The unmapped rest is black. I'm here
to call you out of here. Our mother has
done agnolotti with smoked eggplant and pumpkin.
Medicine-plumped. *Nespole* in a birth bath. In your
underwear—always the spent elastic, the hole in each leg
where you pinch to flatten the fabric under jeans.
I could put a finger through a hole

right now. To the webbing. To thigh. Screw
my body into yours. Speak to you as you.
Would the device change? The poet's call
to no one. Its truth and foolishness and oath.
We used to watch each other play games like this. Watcher more
ashen than controller. From the threshold
I watch an armoury pop like a cat's claw from a pad you were squeezing—
forge sound-effects. More lit map blackens what's veiled
or seems to. No one can cure you. Chanting it powers you.
Agniology: the study of ignorance. Screwed in, I could be the ecstasy

that lets you see your kid self blaze the toboggan run, feel that dawn
-dusk vehemence ribbon the hills with something
let's not call answers. What's unknowable
you can't not know, can't fail to know. I like to think I get it. How it's floor
and ceiling. Build a hospital. Build a cathedral.
A gaol. Build the age's grandest library
for the Goths to sack—every pixel. From those cinders
this hunger. You want matching tattoos.
Nespola trees. Black, with red roots. On the thigh
because we're both looking at your thigh.

Treehouse

What does flinching not decide?
    I spot you into the canopy,
push you by your thighs up through the floor hatch
like raising aloft a chalice.

It mightn't bear our lust long. Look at the rot
in the wall Masonite. Look at how decades of fruit and bat shit bow the roof

my brother and I pitched. A dump. As in a monument
        to the equanimity in leaving
things as they are
that closer sags to neglect, to softer defeat.

Hold me like a higher being who craves without lack. But human, too, a lover
  who holds
crisis
    as currency, barters
fission for access. As if it's not too late. As if the next, closest,

    closeness will contract
like a wave or wave
    patterns on dunes—will specify

while floating formless and nimble. No, what I kept
    from you so I didn't see it wasn't myself. It was the power

that sight had to reveal you in the full swath of your risk.
    As a child, did you billow
a parachute in a hall? Did you sit silly within it?

The sphere of pure loft
          so drum-tight with drag it could never settle—
the settling, the gloving. Touch me sheer. I need you

to spot the misery I stashed here. Need you to help me carry it down
our history. A needle through
          skin, to reach a meridian
it has dulled missing.

Finding Camp at Midnight

Hell in high beams to read
the track's rips—all-wheel-drive
adlibs around ruts, wallows, treefall, echoed
into the earth deep as the one

they follow, the claimed thing, the swirl
the satellites name. Offline
since town, the map can't reroute them. It will lead them
with the last song it remembers

if they're devout carolers. Pricked
for false notes—swerves, arcs, reversals. Struck
-dog glissando of shot brakes. Rocks
beneath the tyres meteors

breaking for windscreen troposphere. If they reach
river, one will adlib, Here—watch
your hands. Orb-weaver. This fabulist
eats by dawn because nature spins

lies to ambush and outlive itself, lets its loveless
rips suck it out to where it can surf itself. If they take
that view, romance it, the thread
of a long harmony will have been machined. The swirling

out-of-into could approach
flush. Trust could bivouac at the red star
like this track dust they taste as it
swims through vents, veins.

Lake

The just-raked gravel outside her room blackens with the black-cockatoo
flock that visits, gossip soft as their yellow cheeks, was that Jupiter
in the sky before the birds, or a satellite, a plane, they're no astronomers, swear on your name
would you eat one, she asks, if you had to eat one to survive could you, if paradise
weren't these big vegan bellies, grapefruit oil in the party-light diffuser, the patterns
in virgin wool and gold-kiwi skin and their feathers through binoculars what hell

would you put one through to stay alive, hit this, well what about her, what hell
is the mere idea, to the brain it's all the same, why do the soft cockatoos
make him cry and condemn them so cocksure, too upset and too cavalier, there's a pattern
here but she can't knit it and don't the birds resemble a solar system, Jupiter
that one meaty one there, bathing in the old wine barrel, they say paradise
is a bird dipping its soft head under cool water, who says that, he says the name

of Dante's first biographer was Villani, can she believe it, see his own name
glinting at the dawn of a language like energy at the birth of a star, a language it's hell
not knowing, a language his father buried under a fig or olive tree to reach the paradise
of monolingualism, of unity, well he's dramatic this evening, speaking to the cockatoos
she's realised he thinks that by not eating animals, by not eating anything metaphorically, Jupiter
next to Earth, he can cause no harm, *go light* as he always says Gary Snyder wrote, pattern

found, pattern knit, well distance-as-kindness has limits, some patterns
neglect's boot prints leave faintly in the dirt, silently, take Jupiter taking the name
and body of Diana to get near Callisto, raping her, chilling post-rape in his Jupiter
power in heaven while Juno throws the pregnant homewrecker into the mud and visits the hell
of disgrace on her, turns her into a bear whom her son kills hunting, won't the cockatoos
find the *nespole* she left on the sill for them, won't they come here, sends to paradise

despite sort of knowing she's more than a bear, she's maybe his mother, and paradise
becomes her, Jupiter turns the slut into Ursa Major, the Great Bear, but that pattern
of starry honour requires her to first be a dead, disgraced bear, one by one black cockatoos
like bearish investors approach the fruit and recoil, why, some chemical, why name
Jupiter the sphere of just rulers, *cherish justice*, Dante knew the myths, he knew Jupiter
in heaven posed Callisto no threat, had he stayed there she might've lived, that's hell

thinking that way, that's cynical, mud as men are, more mud the more godlike, hell
locks from inside, don't they say that, maybe that's as close to a paradise
as she'll ever knit in words, that cliché, she remembers when she thought *Jupiter*
was pronounced *Juniper* and it still rings virtuous, what if distance, the black cockatoos
fly off, weren't the survival his family plotted itself out into, far apart as their good name
ransomed and too far, too far to form a bear, a cockatoo, had this pattern

not knitted his name would the lake between her bicep and elbow be warmer, well
Jupiter can't judge them now, justice has no seat, why not torture hell until
paradise screams, cockatoos, cockatoos, cockatoos, cockatoos, cockatoos, cockatoos

Names for Loquat

Hebrew—*shesek*. A Talmudic word
that may have meant *peach*, or *almond*, or *medlar*.

Here, below our tree, is a bird bath. Every second
summer it fills with fruit that bloats, plums

in syrup, moons in space, my brother in his bunk fever
-saying he's *cold, as an angel, feel*, never

having mentioned angels before, never since.
I melt down the ladder, and there is a king

parrot, no, there are two, eating *pipa*, *naspli*,
lukaat, from the bath

in his ribcage, because this fever has always been
mine to ascribe or suffer here as delight is

abuse when I want it to be, want it to come to light
my nerves' wicks. Some sages called God

a sphere. All centre and no circumference, like brothers playing.
Lovers. Peach scent. What would that make angels—

bibassier, níspero? Say the actual name. Say *nowhere*
as *now here* and tell me it's not fruit. In Lousiana, Sicilians'

niespuli flourished. Today locals
call them *misbeliefs*, and what is truth but a sound

harvest of errors? My favourite, *ameixa amarela*,
means *lovestar*. *Nespola*. *Yellow plum*.

Keepsake

if you do time   take this

that i can't give you

a child   currumbin   first holiday

  brother eager

at mum's breast   near

purple rash

vest legionnaires hat orange floaties

knees in lightning shallows

take deep end rock garden

waterslide   waterfall

take path beyond pool between birds

of paradise banana plants liver

inflorescences to fence

through gate   up palm corridor to sand

  swell

horizon   take this not as

scene   but point of view

see   there is

no child   just attention

near its breast

eager   perfect

Acknowlegements

Thank you to the editors of the publications in which the following poems appear or are forthcoming, sometimes in different versions:

'On the Rise': *Cordite Poetry Review*
'Amateurism (or Youth)': *Action Spectacle* (USA)
'Polyglots': *Action Spectacle* (USA)
'Loquat Giant': *EPOCH* (USA)
'Manifesto': *Verge Anthology*
'Deer Knife': *Australian Book Review*
'Wallpaper': *Australian Book Review*
'Compassionate Grounds': *Cordite Poetry Review*
'Valour': *Cordite Poetry Review*
'Cones': *Action Spectacle* (USA)
'Boulevards': *Australian Poetry Anthology*
'Wish': *Westerly*
'Poison': *Frontier Poetry* (USA)
'Calm Voice': *Best of Australian Poems*
'Athabasca': *Cordite Poetry Review*
'Collecting Brown Matter in Lockdown as the Climate Warms': *Overland*
'When Closing Jackson-Pratt Drains': *The Shore Poetry* (USA)
'Libretti': *Griffith Review*
'Berries': *Westerly*
'Hottest Day of Summer': *Meanjin*
'Dinner Call': *Island Online*
'Names for Loquat': *Australian Poetry Journal*

'Poison' received 3rd place in Frontier Poetry's 2021 Industry Prize.
'Collecting Brown Matter in Lockdown as the Climate Warms' was shortlisted for the 2021 Kuracca Prize for Australian Literature.
'Ulupna Island' was shortlisted in the local category of the 2026 Nillumbik Prize for Contemporary Writing.

'Under the Banner of Heaven' was longlisted for the 2026 Blake Poetry Prize.

Thank you to Shane Strange and Recent Work Press for your continued belief in and support of my work, and Australian poetry. It means more than you know.

Thank you to Creative Australia for providing funding at a pivotal time for this project.

Thank you to Tyler Arnold for lending your artistic gifts, again, to the cover and section breaks of one of my collections.

Deep thanks to Maria, Dominic, and Andy for your blurbs—that is, for your time, and attention.

I'm grateful to Tim Loveday, who read an earlier draft of this manuscript and gave me vital feedback/encouragement.

Emily and Aden, I love you.

I wrote most of this collection on Wurundjeri Country, where storytelling has sustained culture since time immemorial. I pay my respects to Elders and acknowledge that sovereignty was never ceded.

About the Author

Image by Cherry Collins

Anders Villani holds an MFA in Creative Writing from the University of Michigan's Helen Zell Writers' Program, where he received the Delbanco Prize for Poetry, and a PhD from Monash University. He is the author of two previous poetry collections, *Aril Wire* (Five Islands Press, 2018) and *Totality* (Recent Work Press, 2022). Anders' doctoral research investigated poetry's capacity to represent trauma; for work based on his thesis, he received *TEXT Journal*'s 2025 Nigel Krauth Prize.

www.ingramcontent.com/pod-product-compliance
Ingram Content Group Australia Pty Ltd
76 Discovery Rd, Dandenong South VIC 3175, AU
AUHW020611080726
429626AU00003B/4

9 781764 106887